का के की

यह किताब..............................की है।

लेखिका – प्रिया गुप्ता

Copyright © Priya Gupta, 2020
www.hindikaybol.com
All Rights Reserved.
Designed by 'www.arcreativewings.com'

No part of this publication may be reproduced, distributed, or transmitted in any form or by any means, including photocopying, recording, or other electronic or mechanical methods, without the prior written permission of the author, except in the case of brief quotations embodied in critical reviews and certain other non-commercial uses permitted by copyright law.

www.hindikaybol.com
Follow us on FB / IG @ hindikaybol

ISBN Paperback: 978-93-5426-111-4

ISBN Hardcover: 978-93-5915-171-7

To all my students, but foremost my Woodlands batch. For inspiring me to write.

मैं उन सब बच्चों की आभारी हूँ, जिन्होंने मुझे लिखने के लिए प्रेरित किया ।

———————————••• Priya...

सूरज की धूप

गुलाब का फूल

शाम की चाय

बारिश की बूँद

धनक के रंग

मोर के पंख

मटर का पौधा

चिड़िया की चहक

खरगोश के कान

आम की गुठली

गाय का दूध

सुबह की सैर

पेड़ का तना

सेब के बीज

शेर की दहाड़

जंगल का राजा

हाथ का अंगूठा

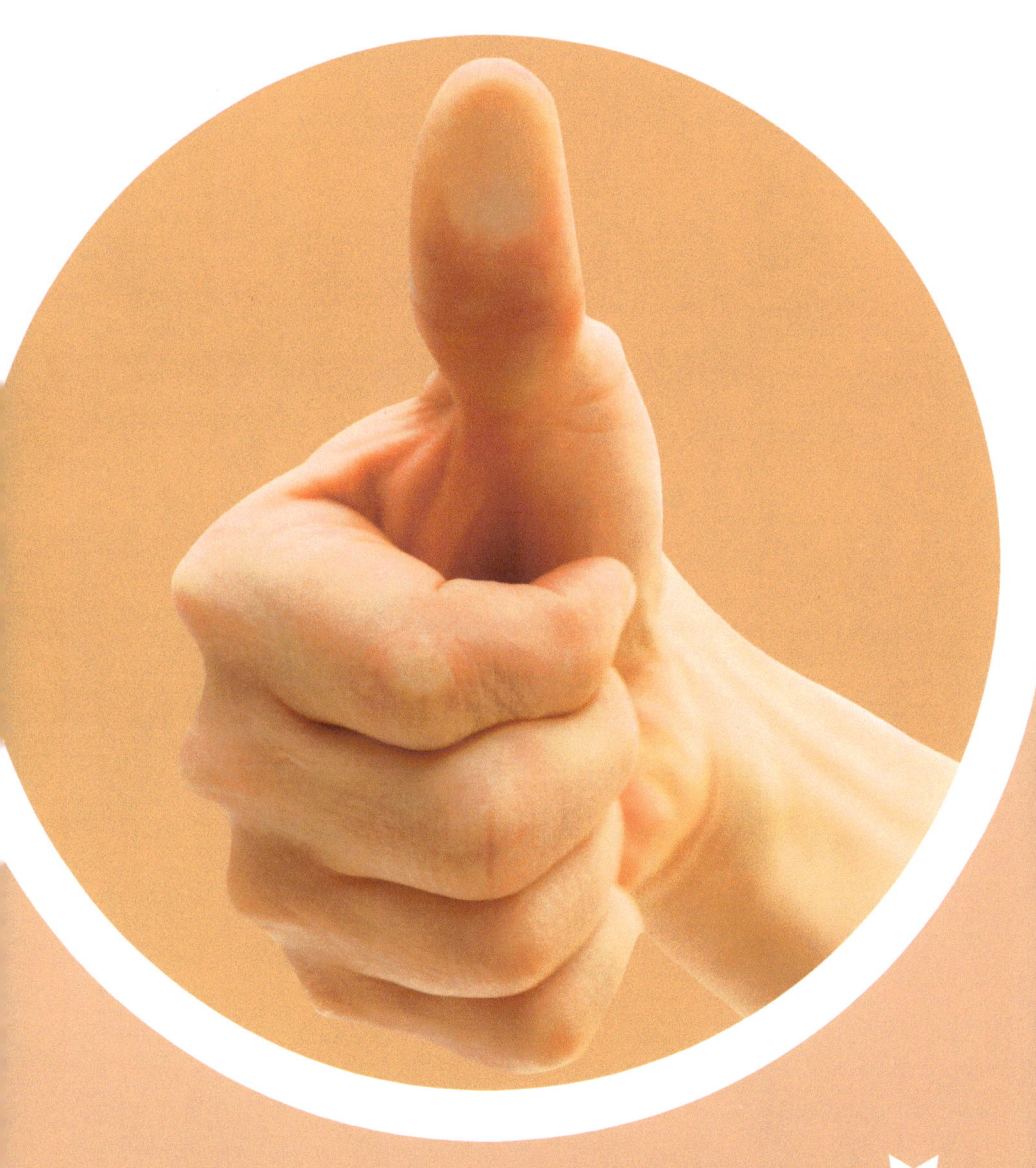

चावल के दाने

A preposition is a word or phrase that connects a noun or pronoun to a verb or adjective in a sentence.

I like the **smell of cake.** Preposition is 'of'.

In Hindi, these words are positioned after the noun/pronoun and hence they are known as post-positions.

Mujhe cake 'की' khushboo pasand hai. Post-position is 'की'.

The postposition का / के / की show a सम्बंध (relation/ belonging) between two words. In English - this is represented by 'of', "'s', and sometimes no word at all.

 'Jar of cookies' will be 'cookies का jar'

'Pumpkin seeds' will be 'pumpkin के seeds'

- 'Bird's beak' will be 'bird की beak'
- 'Morning walk' will be 'morning की walk'

The usage of **का, के** and **की** depends on the gender of the word that belongs, not the word it belongs to. Every noun in Hindi has Masculine (M) or Feminine (F) gender.

Jar is Masculine, so **'का'** is used.

Beak is Feminine, so **'की'** is used.

For Masculine plural (P) words - **'के'** is used, for Feminine plural words, **'की'** is used.

Try the exercise on the next page to build your skills.

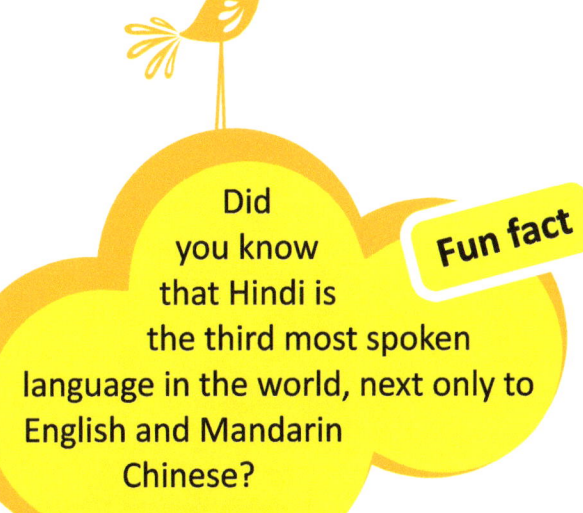

Fun fact

Did you know that Hindi is the third most spoken language in the world, next only to English and Mandarin Chinese?

Sunshine 	 Rose flower	Evening tea 
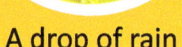 A drop of rain	Colors of the rainbow 	 Feathers of a peacock
Pea plant 	 Chirp of a bird	Rabbit's ears 

Pit of a mango

Cow's milk

Morning walk

Trunk of a tree

Apple seeds

Roar of a tiger

King of the jungle

Thumb

Grains of rice

Try it!

1. राम .... बहन (F/S)
2. होली .... मिठाई (F/S)
3. किताब .... चित्र (M/S/P)
4. हाथ .... जादू (M/S)
5. पापा .... फोन (M/S)
6. पंखे .... हवा (F/S)
7. गाजर .... हलवा (M/S)
8. शेर .... पूँछ (F/S)
9. टमाटर .... बीज (M/S/P)
10. बिल्ली .... आँखे (F/P)

| M is masculine | F is feminine | S is singular | P is plural |

Answer key to exercise

1. का 2. की 3. का/के 4. का
5. का 6. की 7. का 8. की
9. का/के 10. की

The Hindi alphabet

The Hindi alphabet is called वर्णमाला (varnamala) or अक्षरमाला (aksharmala), literally meaning a garland of letters.

It has 13 vowels and 36 consonants.

The consonants combine with vowel markers or मात्रा (matra) to produce different composite letters.

The Hindi script is called Devanagari. Script of a language is the written form of the language.

Vowels / स्वर (swar)

अ	आ	इ	ई	उ	ऊ	ऋ
a	aa	i	ee	u	oo	ri

ए	ऐ	ओ	औ	अं	अः
a	ae	o	au	am	ah

Consonant / व्यंजन (vyanjan)

क	ख	ग	घ	ङ
ka	kha	ga	gh	ng

च	छ	ज	झ	ञ
ca	cha	ja	jha	ña

ट	ठ	ड	ढ	ण
ṭa	ṭha	ḍa	ḍha	ṇa

त	थ	द	ध	न
ta	tha	da	dha	na

प	फ	ब	भ	म
pa	pha	ba	bha	ma

य	र	ल	व
ya	ra	la	va

श	ष	स	ह
sh	sh	sa	ha

क्ष	त्र	ज्ञ
ksh	tra	gya

Vowel sounds explained

Vowel	Sounds like	Vowel Independent Form	Dependent Form (matra)	Dependent Form with Consonant	Sounds like
a	as in about	अ	–	स	as in sun
aa	as in father	आ	ा	सा	as in sour
i	as in bin	इ	ि	सि	as in sit
ee	as in seen	ई	ी	सी	as in see
u	as in book	उ	ु	सु	as in supreme
oo	as in food	ऊ	ू	सू	as in soup
a	as in paid	ए	े	से	as in say
ae	as in mat	ऐ	ै	सै	as in said
o	as in soda	ओ	ो	सो	as in so
au	as in saw	औ	ौ	सौ	as in saw

www.ingramcontent.com/pod-product-compliance
Lightning Source LLC
LaVergne TN
LVHW072322080526
838199LV00112B/488